Anxiety

The Pragmatic Workbook Designed To Assist Individuals In Managing Daily Stress And Anxiety, Promoting Both Physical And Mental Well-Being, Ultimately Leading To A State Of Tranquility

(The Definitive Solution For Alleviating Anxiety And Permanently Treating Panic Attacks)

SabatinoCurcio

TABLE OF CONTENT

Introduction 4

Introduction 1

Physical Well-Being 11

Introduction 25

Overview 43

Rehabilitation: Acknowledging The Actual Situation. 58

Overview Of Cbt...77

Advantages Of Cbt...89

In Conclusion: The Path To Completeness 101

Developing Resilience 120

The Anxiety Powder 127

Recognizing Mental Congestion. 149

Introduction

Introduction

I had recently become a teenager and wasn't big on following trends or dressing like most friends. My wardrobe was so small that I would only buy new clothes when most of the ones I had were completely damaged or no longer fit for wear. You may assume that I was a model thrift or that I supported eco-friendly clothing. These two are not accurate. It was a drastic measure to protect oneself. You see, every time I had to go out in public, my body and mind would react strangely. Whether I was heading to a fantastic restaurant, running errands, or seeing friends, it made no difference.

My body would wake up when a plan was finished, as if trauma was about to happen or was being revisited. My stomach would feel uncomfortable, I would get goosebumps, and I would be unable to move for hours before the incident. My parents were very confused and didn't understand why I was acting this way over what seemed to be a nice event. The addition of judgment to these occurrences made me quite anxious. If we had to go shopping, for instance, I would be thinking of the many salespeople at the store criticizing me for purchasing items of clothing that weren't designed for me or the trial room mirrors reflecting my fears. My anxious mind ignored logic, even though I knew that nobody was interested in my appearance or what I was wearing.

After I believed that I had managed to overcome all the challenges posed by my social anxiety, primarily through staying indoors and avoiding social situations, fate began to play tricks on me. One of my most admirable teachers said I would make a good public speaker. Furthermore, they believed that my best performances would come from situations where I was forced to speak on stage without prior preparation, such as spontaneous speaking competitions. As you may guess, the first few times this plan was attempted, it failed horribly. I would be speechless, anchored to the spot, staring blankly at a group of awkward, sympathetic peers who were also staring back at me. Not unexpectedly, over time, I grew to despise and try to stay away from my favorite teacher. I made every effort to grasp why they insisted on regularly subjecting myself and others to this pain, but I was unable to do so.

But then something changed one day. I was excited about the topic my teacher chose for me, but by then, I had blown it on stage so many times that I was starting to become tired of it. At the time, something else was going on. Everything I had been terrified of, everything I had imagined going wrong, had already materialized. Everyone who knew me had laughed at me, felt sorry for me, and ignored me. I felt centuries had passed before I could recover after freezing on stage. I felt nobody was interested in me anymore, not even in my mistakes.

I only wanted to talk about the matter that was brought up to me that day. My worry didn't go away; it just stopped mattering to me. The day I ended my speech, I was greeted with a tremendous ovation that muffled even my inner critic's now-meek voice. I appreciated the applause, but I realized later that there was something else I enjoyed even more. Many people approached me after my speech to express how much I had touched them and how much my speech had inspired them. I never realized how inspiring she could be to so many people she hardly knew—the little child who got a fever at the mere prospect of conversing with a stranger.

That was the day I decided to connect with new people as much as possible and to start treating my social anxiety seriously. The more these relationships grew, the more I understood the damage my social anxiety was causing to me. For most of my life, I had perceived safety as a limitation. I had become the largest obstacle in living a fulfilling life. My painstakingly constructed "cocoon" had bound me to a life I didn't want.

My previous experiences served as the basis for my current career as a coach and author, where I enjoy assisting clients in resolving issues with confidence and anxiety. I've been trying to figure out how social anxiety works and why it's so hard for people to get over it as adults for years. Numerous people, including myself, have successfully used the techniques discussed in this book to overcome their social anxiety and lead fulfilling lives. While not everyone is fortunate enough to have an incredible teacher like I had, I hope that this book will serve as the roadmap and mentor you require to reach your full potential.

Anyone who believes a social situation invites scorn, criticism, and judgment should read this book. This is for young ladies and girls who find it difficult to recognize their worth in society and believe that to live in peace, they must become smaller or less bright. This is for ladies who have low self-esteem as a result of suppressing and not dealing with their traumas.

This book will help you see things differently if you believe you can never stop the negative self-talk that always runs through your mind. This book can be divided into three sections. We'll study the causes of social anxiety in women as well as how it presents itself in the first section. In the second section, we'll talk about several strategies for overcoming fear and anxiety in social settings, in addition to concentrating on cognitive behavioral therapy (CBT) as a technique for treating social anxiety. The last section will focus on gaining self-assurance and acquiring various skills to successfully negotiate social settings.

You should be able to process any past trauma related to social situations, recognize your triggers and negative thought patterns, gradually build up the confidence to deal with your social anxiety and participate in social situations that you tend to avoid after reading this book.

The ultimate goal is establishing a loving, respectful, and meaningful connection with oneself and others. This book is meant to assist you in viewing yourself as a gift to others, someone who brightens their life only by being. Together, let's begin the next chapter of your incredible life.

Physical Well-Being

Anxiety has negative effects on the body as well as the intellect. For teenagers' general wellbeing wellbeing, it is crucial to comprehend the physical effects of anxiety.

Sleep disturbances: Anxiety can cause sleep disturbances, resulting in insomnia or frequent nighttime awakenings. The ensuing lack of sleep may make anxiety symptoms worse.

Nutritional Impact: Anxiety can cause some teenagers to restrict their diet or turn to comfort eating. These practices may impact both physical health and nutritional intake.

Tension in the muscles and headaches: Anxiety's physical symptoms, such as tense muscles and headaches, can worsen over time, causing discomfort and a reduced quality of life.

Digestive & Stomach Problems: Anxiety is a contributing factor to nausea, upset stomachs, and other digestive issues. The gut-brain axis significantly influences physical symptoms associated with anxiety.

Teens may prioritize their physical health by being aware of the bodily effects of anxiety. This includes adopting relaxation techniques, eating a healthy diet, and regularly exercising.

Part Four: Self-Respect

Teenagers who experience anxiety may see themselves through a skewed lens, which can result in low self-esteem and a negative self-image.

Adolescents who experience anxiety frequently engage in a never-ending cycle of self-criticism, criticizing themselves for what they perceive to be their inadequacies and errors.

Comparing Yourself to Others: Anxiety makes it easier to compare oneself negatively. Adolescents may have feelings of inadequacy or inferiority towards their peers.

Self-Doubt: Anxiety can undermine a person's self-esteem, leading teenagers to question their values and skills. This self-doubt might impede one's ability to grow and succeed.

Dread of Rejection: Anxiety can result in a strong dread of criticism or rejection, which makes it difficult for teenagers to take risks and follow their dreams.

Building resilience and a good self-image requires an understanding of the relationship between anxiety and self-esteem. Teens can learn to accept imperfection as a normal aspect of life, practice self-compassion, and confront negative self-talk.

The intelligence theory of Robert Sternberg

American psychologist Robert Sternberg created the second theory of intelligence

I would like to discuss with you. His intelligence theory, known as the "triarchical theory of intelligence" or "tripartite theory," was developed. It highlights the three dimensions of intelligence: practical, creative, and analytical.

Traditional IQ tests mostly evaluate analytical intelligence. IQ measures what is often known as logical-mathematical intelligence. This kind of intellect is associated with manipulating logical symbols, solving logical or mathematical problems, and abstract reasoning. Since it nearly exactly duplicates the logical and mathematical intelligence you are already familiar with, I won't waste too much time on this kind of intelligence. I would rather go on to the next intelligence category because of this.

Conversely, creative intelligence refers to the capacity for novel and creative problem-solving. Even in everyday speech, words like "originality" and "creativity" are frequently used. That's right—creative intelligence is the exact type of intellect that allows us to describe someone as imaginative and capable of coming up with novel solutions to challenging issues. These days, workplaces are taking more and more consideration of creative intelligence. For instance, you may have already heard of soft talents during job interviews. Sternberg coined "creative intelligence," which encompasses a wide range of soft talents. As you can see, many of us already know that there are intelligences other than logical-mathematical or rational intelligence, even if we are unfamiliar with Sternberg's theory.

Last but not least, Sternberg proposed the existence of a type of intelligence he dubbed "practical intelligence." It has to do with the capacity to adjust and apply knowledge gained to real-world scenarios encountered in daily life. People with this intelligence can frequently solve complicated problems using only their bodies and specific procedures rather than abstract reasoning. A highly skilled person in this area may struggle to grasp concepts and use abstract reasoning, but he or she excels at solving problems that call for practical methods and abilities. Unfortunately, we mistakenly associate "knowing how to do" with a non-intelligent practical competence too frequently. On the other hand, according to Sternberg, one of the types of intelligence is the ability to perform.

I want to share one more pertinent fact before I end this paragraph. In contrast to Gardner, Sternberg did not believe that various forms of intelligence were distinct, autonomous entities. Sternberg believed that the three types of intellect were in communication with one another without becoming too specific. To give just one example, those who are practically endowed typically possess the ability to think creatively, provided that they apply their reasoning to tangible situations rather than abstract ones. I can now officially declare that you have finished reading the second chapter. You now know the main relevant ideas of these two well-known theories of intelligence. Now, all you have to do is turn the page and finally explore the subject of emotional intelligence! It is, after all, the most significant section of this book.

Attaining mental and physical wellbeing requires tranquility and optimistic thinking.

In examining the function of good ideas, we must uphold the essentiality of tranquility and positive thinking for attaining mental and physical wellbeing. You must consider the mind and body to be in continual communication with one another because of the strong connections between the two. You must nurture positive thinking and pursue tranquility daily to attain true mental and physical wellbeing. Twellbeingdwellbeinge is a very intimate relationship developed daily; therefore, keeping balance by leading a disciplined life only a few days a week will not help. You must ensure complete consistency if you truly wish to live in harmony and enable mind and body to work together constructively. Your immune system is impacted by stress and negative thoughts, as I said in the last section. That's why you could get sick more easily during intense stress. Try not to think negatively if you want to prevent this harm to your equilibrium, both mentally and physically.

On the other hand, having positive ideas is crucial to reaching both physical and mental wellbeing since they improve your mood, lower stress levels, and increase resilience or your ability to withstand setbacks in life. As a result, we may effectively handle stress, keep a positive outlook, and preserve our physical and mental well-being and well-being thinking. Conversely, serenity enables us to properly manage our emotions and remain composed under pressure.

There are numerous techniques for developing happy thinking and, consequently, dispelling negative ones. Throughout all five books in this bundle, I will give you lots of advice on how to start thinking positively and concentrate your mental and physical health on yourself. I want to start by saying that you should never undervalue the importance of a balanced diet and regular exercise. Even though they may initially seem difficult. Our bodies require an average of three months to acclimate to a diet or habit that differs from our usual ones. Because of this, wait at least three months before making dietary changes if you don't observe any improvement. If not, you might not get what you wanted since you didn't wait long enough!

Lastly, I want you to remember this idea: I'm talking about the value of social ties. You must pay close attention to developing solid and fulfilling social ties to maintain mental and physical equilibrium. This is very essential! Your brain needs interpersonal relationships to receive adequate stimulation to communicate with your body and undergo self-modification. Thus, it is reasonable to say that preserving positive interpersonal interactions is crucial to a person's physical and mental stability. I think you understand all I intended to say regarding the significance of thinking positively for reaching psychophysical wellbeing. You are now going to concentrate on the final chapter of this second book, in which I will provide useful tips and techniques for mastering the power of your mind.

Introduction

Notice: This book's data is mainly for general informational purposes. Despite great care and attention to detail in creating the content, the author disclaims all responsibility for any mistakes or omissions, whether direct or indirect. Although the advice and techniques in this book might be useful for enhancing mental health, they shouldn't be used in place of expert psychological assistance. The author advises anyone experiencing anxiety, depression, or other mental health issues to get help from a licensed mental health practitioner. It is recommended that readers who have concerns regarding their mental health speak with a certified therapist or counselor or their doctor.

Worry and anxiety seem to be a part of our busy daily lives. Stress intensifies until it seems barriers are closing in, suffocating clarity and inner serenity. You can't sleep at night because your mind is constantly racing. You rush from crisis to crisis without breaking, and your nerves fray. Daily obstacles appear enormous. When you think of facing them all, panic swells in your chest.

You are familiar with the oppressive pressure and racing thoughts. Anxiety robs life of its vitality, making even easy tasks difficult. An ongoing state of agitation saps the vital energy needed to live completely. Your brain obsesses on issues without offering solutions. Your body is constantly producing stress chemicals that prevent you from relaxing and allowing you to remain in a fight-flight-freeze state.

Take heart if this exhausting feeling of perpetual tension seems familiar to you. You can get long-lasting relief, and you are not alone. This book provides a wide range of evidence-based, holistic methods that have been demonstrated to calm anxiety and concern from the inside out. They allow you to change thoughts, calm frazzled nerves, and increase inner resilience.

Think of this book as your guide, illuminating a route to tranquility you might not be aware exists out of the dark forests of anxiety. Every chapter presents a method supported by research, explains how to use it and why it works, and offers more information and advice. Consider these as additional resources for your mental health toolbox. Try them carefully and patiently. As you practice consistently, anxiety's hold on you weakens, and you start to regain a sense of possibilities, joy, and peace that was previously hidden.

These pages provide 34 methods science has proven to effectively lessen stress and anxiety. The chapters incorporate the most recent research in psychology and holistic health, which range from utilizing deep breathing to trigger the relaxation response to employing cognitive behavioral therapy to restructure thought patterns to using music to calm the senses. Studies supporting each technique show that it can improve general mental well-being, promote cognitive clarity, and soothe the body and mind. Consider this guide an unlimited array that lets you try various strategies. Decide what best suits your requirements and tastes, then commit to a customized regimen using the most effective techniques. With 43 tried-and-true methods at your disposal, you can take your time finding the perfect anxiety-reduction toolset for your body, mind, and way of life.

It takes bravery to look beyond a person's old fear and follow new directions until they become reliable lifelines to heal. But it feels liberated to take that first move. You begin rewiring ingrained patterns to produce more beneficial reactions. Confidence grows with every little accomplishment. As worry begins to lessen its hold on you, you experience more optimism, lightness, and vitality throughout the day. You stop letting continual fear hold you back and start to open up to the beauties and opportunities of life.

The chapters cover a wide range of strategies, including mental, physical, social, artistic, and more, so you may customize your "anxiety wellness routine" by implementing the particular methods that work best for you. You'll find your perfect routines and practices via trial and error—routines that work well to ease anxiety symptoms and fit into your everyday schedule. Remain adaptable as requirements and abilities evolve with time. You will have many tools in this book to adjust as circumstances demand.

Rather than being a quick remedy, anxiety healing is a journey with ups and downs. Have perseverance and patience. Have faith in your innate power and deservingness of tranquility. You should not be overtaken with worry; you should feel connected, stable, and hopeful. If you apply these techniques consistently, anxiety will gradually become less of a hold on you. Through self-compassion and the guidance of this expert, you will gradually recapture your sense of constant serenity, joy, and clarity. If you can muster the guts to look for it, there is a path out into the light. So let's get started. The first step is taking a deep breath and allowing yourself to be open to good transformation via regular practice. You provide the willingness; this book offers the guide and daily motivation. Together, we'll let go of outdated myths, unhelpful cognitive patterns, and ingrained physiological reactions that lead to worry. There will be challenges, but you will gain resilience, wisdom, and self-awareness with each you conquer.

This is your life, your path. With the tools, you may regain control and guide your mental state toward possibilities and serenity. Maintain your daily focus, have trust, and allow these techniques to illuminate the way so that you can begin truly living once more. If you are dedicated to the process, the fog will clear. This is something you can handle. Now, take a deep breath, and let's begin.

What should you do if you suffer from trauma?

Start by locating qualified expert assistance. When you can pinpoint the initial trauma, the underlying limiting belief, and a practical, empowering belief to take its place, you're on your way to transformation.

Every successful intervention consists of four steps. You can utilize them to transform the traumas under the guidance of a qualified and supportive mentor.

The first step is the most difficult. The more strongly the trauma memories elicit strong emotional reactions, the more effective it is at locating the sensory memory of the trauma and the limiting belief that goes along with it. Given that this occurs frequently at random, why not investigate it? However, don't attempt this unless you have access to reliable external and internal resources, such as knowledgeable, trustworthy people and a secure environment to which you can retreat if necessary, both in your mind and the real world. The awakened trauma memory is using your working memory, and it needs to be fully engaged for your unconscious mind to handle it in the next step with the least amount of suffering.

It is possible to remove unhealthy belief circuits and rewire the brain with more constructive beliefs when one knows how to trigger the belief circuits and the accompanying emotions. Our belief systems—software—about the world and ourselves have the power to either empower or constrain us. Strong, restricting ideas frequently take control of our conduct after trauma.18 This level can be significantly impacted by trauma resolution therapies that are effective.

The next step is to come to your senses using distraction, such as refocusing on a genuine sensory experience in the present, to break the circuit of triggered trauma.19 An additional choice is to attempt patterned alternate motions like running in place, dancing, or back-and-forth eye movements. Doing this breaks the working memory circuit, enabling your brain to quickly and automatically start processing the trauma without conscious intervention. Even if you can only initially divert yourself for 15 seconds, strive to do so for 15 minutes after lighting up the distressing memory. The next step is to connect with the internal and external resources you already have access to, which would have given you a sense of security, worth, control, etc. This can be as easy as realizing that you are a survivor and not a victim or as easy as visualizing yourself receiving the assistance you require or would provide for yourself right now. Ironically, the most helpful resource for internalizing limiting ideas linked with trauma is often a fictitious character who can offer protection, a sense of worth or control, or a good message or belief in place of the restricting ones. This is where a professional therapist's dyadic resourcing can be extremely beneficial.[20]

The final phase is to picture yourself utilizing your newly acquired resourcefulness and abilities should future encounters with situations or occurrences cause your traumatic reactions.

Your well-being is the most important thing you can accomplish. You can help people more when you are healthy and have mastered the art of problem-solving, even if it's just by serving as an example of how to live a contented and fruitful life. This has a significantly bigger impact on the world than most people realize.

What comes next?

Amazing researchers and doctors around the world are reducing the causes and effects of child trauma. What if all child welfare and juvenile justice systems could alter children, teenagers, and caregivers by working together to duplicate tiny, extremely successful pilot initiatives anywhere? What if it is extended to everyone who wants and needs it because it lowers long-term costs at every level and benefits the most vulnerable? You would support it to the best of your ability, wouldn't you?

The seven-year-old, who was oppositional, rebellious, distractible, impulsive, extremely traumatized, and emotionally unstable, is now nine years old and continues to gain from the therapies mentioned above. He is secure and happy, doing well in school, and has moved past the pain of his early life. The best part is that he is excited "all in" as he starts a new life with a wonderful "forever family."

And the killer within the Plexiglass enclosure? William Bonin was the notorious Freeway Killer, a man who killed at least twenty-one boys and men in his youth. I was in that cage with him for three days in a row, performing a neuropsychiatric assessment and wondering what could lead to such catastrophic consequences. What was going through this monster's mind?

Stacks of historical records from his past—child protective services, family descriptions, mental health, and medical records, records from his placement in an orphanage, school records, juvenile justice placements, military records, previous prison records—and testimonies from people who knew him in different placements and schools—were examined every evening in an attempt to piece together his development.

Upon eventually aligning everything, it was heartbreaking to look back and see all the chances lost that could have averted the catastrophic results. Even more challenging was when I underwent the "phenomenological reduction" and "got into his head," experiencing his twisted, vindictive desire for someone to comprehend the helplessness and terror he had experienced as a child and to be able to hold onto those experiences forever, free from betrayals like those who testified against him and led to previous imprisonments.

After meeting with Bonin, I needed many weeks to recuperate as I was the initial one among numerous death row assessments that followed. Bill Bonin was put on San Quentin's Death Row and executed by lethal injection at a cost of about $12 million, including the appeals process. My encounter with him has inspired me to work toward improving the lives of wounded kids.

Overview

The winds of life are fierce and unforgiving in today's world of constant change, and they can seem to be working against us. Depression and anxiety are all too frequent; they loom over us like unrelenting storm clouds, waiting to swallow us in their violent grasp. The pressure to succeed and uphold an illusion of perfection can leave us feeling lost and overburdened as we traverse the turbulent waves of life. But have no fear—there are rays of hope even amid the darkest skies, and we may find the strength to sail against the current even in the harshest storms.

As the story continues, I want you to know I know your daily challenges. Even while it may seem like you are the only one going through anxiety and sadness at times, you are not. Even with the people in your life, it's normal to feel misinterpreted or abandoned, which exacerbates emotional pain. Rest assured, we can navigate this turbulent sea together because numerous others have experienced similar storms.

The most important thing you might face is how hard it is to balance your everyday obligations and life. Even the easiest chores might become overwhelmed by the shadow of anxiety and despair. It's critical to understand that this battle is a testimonial to the ferocity of the storm you are riding out, not a reflection of your incompetence.

Anxious and depressed people may experience crippling fear and anxiety about the future. Worst-case scenarios could always replay in your head, making you feel uneasy. In the meantime, depression may obstruct your ability to see into the future and make it tough to imagine a better day. Relieving the weight of future uncertainty and enabling you to fully appreciate it.

Your sense of worth and self-esteem may suffer greatly as a result of your struggle with anxiety and depression. Your mind may be filled with self-defeating ideas that make you feel unworthy of happiness or like a burden to everyone around you. These beliefs do not define you; therefore, don't worry.

Even if you've tried coping mechanisms in the past, it can be difficult to identify or put into practice healthy ones. Realizing that there isn't a single answer that works for everyone is essential. We shall examine various coping strategies in this book and assist you in customizing them to your requirements and situation.

Life is a journey that frequently takes us through choppy seas; occasionally, we find ourselves cruising through stormy waters. It is crucial to understand that overcoming these obstacles is not a sign of weakness but a necessary component that transforms us into better, more knowledgeable people. Recognize that you are not alone in your struggle with anxiety and depression and that asking for assistance is a sign of courage and strength rather than weakness.

This book will discuss many advantages, all of which will work together to make your life less stressful and purposeful. We will both gain a great deal, some of which are as follows:

● Realizing and normalizing your experience: You will find comfort in this book when you realize that you are not alone in your difficulties with depression and anxiety. We hope to normalize your experience by bringing attention to these common mental health issues and dispelling any guilt or embarrassment you may be feeling.

● Empowerment in asking for assistance: It can be difficult, but it is a brave gesture that can bring about significant change. This book encourages you to recognize the power of asking for help from friends and family to outside experts. You'll be inspired to reach out without holding back because doing so is a show of strength rather than weakness.

● Useful coping techniques: "Navigating the Storm" provides a variety of practical coping techniques to assist you in navigating the storms of sadness and anxiety. These tools, which range from self-compassion exercises to mindfulness methods, will allow you to take control of your emotional health and create peaceful moments even in the middle of stress.

● Overcoming emotions of loneliness: You will come to understand that you are not traveling alone as you go through this guide. You can overcome the sense of loneliness that anxiety and depression frequently impose by learning from the experiences of others who have faced comparable struggles. This can help you feel connected and at ease.

● Accepting both the present and the future: It can be incredibly transforming to learn to live in the now and let go of worries about the future. "Navigating the Storm" will provide you with self-grounding techniques to maintain hope and optimism throughout uncertain times.

● Boosting self-worth and self-esteem: This book will guide you through low self-esteem and self-doubt. You will develop a good self-image and realize your genuine value through self-compassion and introspection, giving you the confidence you need to face the outside world.

Motivating development and adaptability: Ultimately, "Navigating the Storm" is a manual for development and resiliency. As you go through its chapters, you will be motivated to rise to problems head-on and see them as chances for growth and development.

You'll learn priceless perspectives, individualized plans, and empirically supported techniques for controlling your emotions and taking back command of your life. Take the initiative now and start this path toward a better life instead of waiting for the storm to pass.

This book's pivotal moment is based on a life-changing experience led by the S.T.O.R.M.S. model, a systematic and individualized strategy for treating depression and anxiety. With the help of this potent model, you will be able to face life's obstacles head-on and gain the skills necessary to weather any emotional storm that comes your way.

Spot, Tame, Opt, Reduce, Modify, and Shape are the acronym for S.T.O.R.M.S., each of which stands for a critical component in your journey toward better mental health and well-being. These elements create a comprehensive framework to help you develop resilience and greet life with newfound vitality. What precisely is S.T.O.R.M.S. then? Let's investigate!

Remember that not everyone will exhibit all these symptoms and that every person's experience is different.

4. Disproportionality of Chemicals

Chemical imbalance is both a cause and an effect of anxiety, a mild but powerful undercurrent in the complex processes of the human brain. It is evidence of the fine balance necessary for the best possible mental health and the complex interactions between neurotransmitters, receptors, and synapses that can tip the scales in favor of anxiety.

A disturbance in the balance of neurotransmitters, which are chemical messengers that let brain cells communicate, is the fundamental cause of this disorder. For instance, serotonin is essential for controlling mood. Anxiety is one of the emotions that can arise from an imbalance in serotonin levels.

Think of serotonin as the conductor of an orchestra, directing the brain's ensemble's emotions and reactions.

Anxiety and discordant emotions might take center stage when the conductor falters and there isn't enough serotonin to create harmony. This chemical imbalance can cause persistent anxiety, restlessness, or even panic attacks.

Moreover, serotonin isn't the only neurotransmitter in this complex dance. Other neurotransmitters, including norepinephrine and dopamine, also influence anxiety. A norepinephrine imbalance can cause a condition of increased attention and alarm, whereas an excess of dopamine might cause hypervigilance and heightened arousal.

Chemical imbalance is a complex cause and trigger of anxiety because it can both cause and exacerbate the disorder.

It may be a genetic predisposition that paves the way for anxiety disorders in the future.

Furthermore, outside variables such as stress, trauma, or substance misuse can upset this delicate balance even more, strengthening the grip of anxiety or causing it to arise.

Realizing how a physiological imbalance contributes to worry serves as a reminder of how intricate mental health is. It emphasizes the necessity of a comprehensive strategy for diagnosis and therapy, one that considers the complex chemistry of the brain and psychological and environmental variables.

Understanding that a chemical imbalance does not indicate frailty or failure is critical. Similar to variances in physical health, it's a normal diversity in brain chemistry. Similar to how we seek medical attention for physical illnesses, treating chemical imbalances in anxiety frequently includes using coping mechanisms, therapy, and drugs that restore equilibrium.

In the vast array of factors that contribute to and provoke anxiety, chemical imbalance plays a prominent role. That's evidence of the complexity of the human brain and the significant impact that subtle chemical interactions can have on our emotional health. Knowing how these factors interact enables people to look for efficient therapies and successfully negotiate the challenging landscape of anxiety while maintaining hope and resilience.

Rehabilitation: Acknowledging The Actual Situation.

After being away for so long, Charles was excited to finally go home. He felt well on the way back and managed to get some sleep in the ambulance, something he had not been able to accomplish in the two months following the accident. His mother and uncle joined him, and he felt at ease since he thought everything would soon return to normal. Charles was welcomed home by a group of people excited to see him when the ambulance door opened. It felt good to be warmly welcomed, as though he had just won the World Cup and was going home with the trophy.

He went home to find friends who played soccer and friends who used to skate with him. Despite the excitement, Charles desired nothing more at that moment than his room and bed. The hospital setting, with all the equipment and the stench of sterilization, was getting old to me. He wanted to lie on his stomach, the way he always slept, and pick up his blanket, which was so worn out that it fit his body perfectly. He also wanted to locate his sneakers damaged from walking so much, his skateboard propped up next to the bed, and the room's distinct smell. But when Charles got to his room, he had a bad surprise in store.

After being wheeled to his room, he saw another hospital bed when he got there. Nothing remained of what she remembered before leaving the house on the day of the accident; her room had been completely changed. His old footwear, his skateboard, and the stench of his feet that had formerly filled the entire room were all gone. Instead, there was just a television, a sterile room, and a bed that looked like it belonged in an intensive care unit. Charles felt a wave of disappointment as if he had landed at a different hospital.

Charles lived in an area so pristine that mosquitoes had to apply hand sanitizer before they could fly over it. As a result, he began to experience more frequent episodes of severe despair and anxiety, which were exacerbated by other parts of the new reality he had to accept. Day by day, the weight of all that had transpired began to sink in, and Charles realized he was not mentally ready to handle it all. Who, after all, would be?

The inability to travel around as he pleased was an intolerable burden. He yearned for his leg motions to just grab his skateboard and get out of that atmosphere filled with the stench of alcohol and the sorrowful expressions on people's faces upon witnessing him in that predicament. Because of the stitches from the spinal surgery, it was essential to move his room to give him the best care and prevent infection. However, all the twelve-year-old wanted was his life to return to its previous state.

It seemed like a truck ran over his mental health with every fresh reality check. The worst part was that Charles was finding it difficult to resist the psychological damage brought on by the repercussions of his new world. He was becoming increasingly like a sinkhole, and the sense of powerlessness that accompanied these difficulties was starting to overwhelm him.

After another nearly sleepless night, Charles awoke at dawn on his first day home to find someone had invaded his room. Daniela was her name, and she would serve as his physical therapist for the ensuing few months. After spending time with Daniela, Charles quickly concluded that women can act calm and collected while intentionally causing pain to someone. He saw her that way while she tormented him with the stretches.

Charles would scream and weep in agony as soon as she arrived, taking her pillow to place on her face and begin the exercises. He realized the discomfort was warranted since he hadn't moved a muscle from his waist down for two months. Any movement hurt so much, no matter how little. They had hired a specialist to start physical therapy sessions as soon as he returned from the first leg of his medical adventure since it was essential to prevent muscular atrophy.

Even though he is thankful for Daniela and the physical treatment now, his urge to vent his pain, sorrow, and wrath on someone was further heightened by his daily workout sessions back then. Charles didn't realize, though, just how much he would have to overcome or that the discomfort he was experiencing from his physiotherapy was just the start of a protracted struggle.

Charles's misery didn't end with the anguish he experienced during physical therapy. He had to deal with equally agonizing post-physical therapy symptoms after every session. The exercises activated his nervous system, resulting in shocks to his leg muscles that felt like cramps. The position and intensity of these aches varied; at times, they were like excruciating torture, and they fluctuated based on both physical and emotional variables.

Charles could not apply pressure to the place that hurt to relieve the agony, unlike most persons who cannot move. The aches tormented him nonstop as he lay pinned to his bed. The worst aspect was that these pains were in areas of his body, like his foot, where he had lost sensation. Similar to how menstrual cramps might impact a woman's mood, Charles's mental state suffered as a result of these ongoing shocks because nobody can be joyful when experiencing pain all the time.

Charles and the doctors did not entirely understand the source of these unbearable aches, but they started as soon as physical therapy was started. Daniela's physiotherapist argued that these symptoms indicated that his muscles responded to the therapy. But after going through these excruciating symptoms for a week, Charles lost his patience. The post-physiotherapy pains were getting intolerable, especially at night when he was attempting to sleep, so he didn't see the point in continuing. He became so filled with hate and frustration that he started to rebel and stopped talking to his family and the physical therapist. It was his method of expressing his dissatisfaction with the circumstances.

Charles was lost in a whirlwind of unpleasant feelings, anguish, and rage consuming him. He didn't see why he should put himself through so much pain, especially since physical therapy was meant to be beneficial to him anyway. He started to distance himself from everyone around him, even his mother, who had always loved and cared for him deeply, and silence became his only mode of protest.

As the months passed, Charles started to absorb all of this pain and rage. He allowed his emotions and his suffering to fester inside of him and stopped discussing them. His psychological state deteriorated due to the lack of communication; he even entertained thoughts of ending his own life as a means of escaping his agony since it seemed that no one genuinely understood or cared about him.

His mother never gave up on him despite everything. Even though it was impossible, she went above and beyond to give Charles some semblance of well-being. Because of his compromised immunity, his mother was constantly taking care of him and doing everything she could to prevent any chance of infection, from setting up the room for his arrival to enforcing stringent hygiene measures on those who visited. She was her son's strongest ally and guardian, always putting her son's needs first. The welfare of her son has always been Charles's mother's top priority. She has taken precautions since he was a youngster to make sure his health issues do not cause him to become stunted. She showed Charles her unwavering affection by hiring Daniela, a physiotherapist, to complete daily exercises.

Charles hoped he could travel back in time as he grew older and reflected on his history. Even though she was silent and had a shuttered countenance because of the grief he was carrying, he recalled the moments when his mother would come into his room and show him love and attention. He desperately wanted to tell her that everything would be alright and that his mother was the one who inspired him to keep fighting.

Charles realized the great price his mother had paid to care for him and give up her life. He thought back to the times he was angry that he was still alive and chose not to answer his mother's questions about how things were going. His thoughts were consumed by an ongoing fight that alternated between his need to avoid burdening his family and his weariness from suffering.

Charles gradually descended into a profound condition of anxiety and despair. He refused guests and avoided socializing, in addition to getting little sleep, eating poorly, and isolating himself from everyone. The one constant in her life was her physiotherapy sessions with Daniela, who, despite her resilience, recognized the need for exercise to aid her recovery. In addition to facing many physical and mental difficulties, Charles' journey was characterized by his mother Clara's unwavering love and dedication, which kept her from giving up on him even in the face of despair.

Anxiety is excessive worry about everything, while depression is defined by apathy towards life. These illnesses don't require severe trauma to affect a person. People occasionally realize that their lives appear out of control and that the things they once loved no longer have any purpose.

Teens and older children are typically affected by social anxiety

Helping kids who struggle with social anxiety

By learning to comprehend your child's anxiety, you can help them as much as possible. Keeping an eye out for your child's anxiety symptoms and the circumstances in which they appear is a useful strategy. Over time, patterns may become apparent if these indications and circumstances are documented.

There are various strategies to support your child after you have a better understanding of their social anxiety.

Before Daycare, Education, or Additional Social Situations

1. Get them ready: It's like giving your child a toolkit for life's obstacles—preparing them for the things that make them anxious or afraid. You can set up a secure area at home where you two can role-play these situations and work out solutions. It's similar to practicing for a show, where your kids can hone their abilities and gain self-assurance in managing certain circumstances. By this proactive approach, they are equipped with useful skills, which makes navigating social problems easier.

2. Promote Critical Thinking: Giving your youngster a magnifying glass to critically examine their nervous thoughts is

analogous to encouraging "detective thinking." Ask them politely, "How do you know they'll laugh?" if they're worried about anything, such as fearing the class would laugh at them. It's similar to teaching kids to conduct independent investigations and look for hints and proof. In this manner, individuals can confront those uneasy ideas and determine whether they are grounded in reality or just products of their imagination. It is an effective strategy for boosting their self-assurance and fortifying them against social anxiety.

3. Talk About Your Own Experiences: Giving your child a helpful road map can be achieved by discussing your own

experiences of experiencing social anxiety and how you overcame your worries. It enables kids to realize that talking about nervous feelings is normal and acceptable in everyday situations. By demonstrating to them that worry can be understood and controlled, your honesty can act as an encouraging role model, giving them the confidence to talk about their feelings and a sense of comfort.

4. Let the preschool or school know: Opening a window to let in sunlight when you let your child's preschool or school know about their anxiousness is the same. Giving them a road plan to better understand and help your child is akin to sharing what you're doing to

support them. It takes teamwork to enable teachers and staff to give your kid a stable and supportive environment. In this manner, everyone is cooperating to establish a secure environment where your child can flourish despite their anxiety difficulties.

Recognizing and treating social anxiety in kids is essential to assisting them in interacting with others more comfortably and confidently. Through preemptive measures and encouraging candid dialogue, you can offer your child invaluable assistance in overcoming their social anxiety obstacles.

Overview Of Cbt

Cognitive behavioral therapy: what is it?

Definition and Foundations

CBT, or cognitive behavioral therapy, is more than a psychological catchphrase. This well-researched, empirically supported type of psychotherapy seeks to identify and reframe harmful thinking patterns to influence the feelings and actions that these beliefs elicit. Despite the abundance of classifications, the main premise is that CBT enables you to comprehend how your ideas, feelings, and behaviors are interrelated. It provides a proactive, useful approach to mental health by breaking down the intricate workings of human psychology into manageable parts.

It is a common misconception that CBT involves "positive thinking." It addresses the dysfunctional thoughts rather than asking you to eliminate the negative ones. CBT differs from more conventional, exploratory therapies like psychoanalysis in that it has a clear emphasis on this area. While the latter could explore the reasons behind your early experiences, CBT focuses on the "here and now." The goal is to provide you with the tools you need to properly handle your mental condition right now. CBT uses a toolbox of tactical methods, each one specifically crafted to address a particular psychological issue. These can include "Exposure and Response Prevention," "Behavioral Experiments," and "Thought Records." The worst part is this: CBT has no "one size fits all" strategy. Technique selection usually ensures a customized treatment plan by considering each individual's goals, context, and specific challenges.

Let's examine a few of its components more closely:

All-encompassing Nature: CBT doesn't function in isolation. It considers the whole spectrum of human experience, including behavioral repercussions, emotional triggers, and cognitive distortions.

Goal-Oriented: Every workout or session is planned with a certain goal, making the progress discernible and the process measurable.

Self-Empowering: CBT's emphasis on self-efficacy may be its most alluring feature. It enhances resilience throughout life by teaching you the techniques to become your therapist.

Flexible and Adaptable: CBT is adaptable to online platforms and group situations and has many applications.

In the following chapters, we will explore CBT's specific applications, historical development, and procedures in more detail. Therefore, it is important to understand these fundamental features. We'll look at what makes it unique and practical ways you may use it to enhance your life.

Understanding the principles presented in this chapter prepares you for a life-changing adventure into cognitive behavioral therapy, which offers real, long-lasting change and insight.

Use in Therapy: Cognitive behavioral therapy, or CBT, has become more well-known due to its applicability and efficacy, especially in clinical settings. Although understanding the fundamentals of CBT is crucial—as covered in the part before this one—the real action happens when we talk about its therapeutic uses. This part will examine how CBT is implemented differently from other therapeutic approaches and why that difference is important.

The First Evaluation

An initial examination that functions as a diagnostic interview is usually the first step in CBT. But unlike conventional therapies, which require the patient to spend multiple sessions reliving their past, CBT looks for present problems that negatively impact the patient's quality of life. Here, the therapist acts more like a coach, helping you recognize the patterns in your feelings, ideas, and actions. Because the emphasis is always on the "here and now," the preliminary assessment is essential to creating a schedule for upcoming meetings.

The Healing Partnership

Developing a cooperative relationship is essential in all treatments, but in cognitive behavioral therapy (CBT), the client and therapist collaborate to set particular goals. These objectives are frequently SMART (Specific, Measurable, Achievable, Relevant, and Time-bound) to monitor development and make necessary modifications. Because of its goal-oriented methodology, CBT is notably proactive. CBT is a two-way, interactive conversation in which both participants take responsibility for the other's success, in contrast to therapies that cast the expert as an objective, detached spectator.

Structure of Sessions

Another distinction is the distinct format of CBT sessions. A session usually starts with summarizing the previous week's activities and homework. However, most of the session is devoted to using the right CBT approaches to analyze the client's specific problem. After the class, fresh homework assignments are typically assigned. This systematic approach guarantees that every session is fruitful and that the therapist and client are both aware of the progress that has been accomplished.

Assignments: The Field of Practice

CBT indeed involves homework, and this isn't a mistake. Like thinking journals or behavioral studies, homework assignments are meant to apply the knowledge acquired in therapy to practical situations. CBT integrates the lessons learned into your everyday life, unlike alternative therapeutic models that could limit the therapeutic experience to the consulting room's four walls. This ongoing cycle of doing, learning, and reflecting is a special use of CBT that increases its efficacy.

Individualization

Though CBT is usually applied individually, its principles apply to all situations. A special set of methods is used after determining the fundamental problems. The methods are customized to meet each client's needs, whether through a Thought Record for someone struggling with a phobia or Exposure Therapy for someone overcoming recurrent negative self-talk.

Succinct yet intense

The duration of CBT is another important factor to consider, as it is typically shorter than other treatment approaches. Depending on the topic's complexity, a typical course could take six to twenty sessions. Even while it can seem short, each session's intensity and focus can result in noticeable changes in a short amount of time.

CBT is precise, goal-driven, systematic, and intensively focused on practical application in the therapeutic environment. These features make it a great tool for addressing various mental health concerns and giving you the tools to better manage life's obstacles, as you will learn in the upcoming chapters.

Section 1

You can practice CBT on your own or with assistance from a specialist. If you choose to see a therapist, you will almost certainly have homework. During your sessions, you will discuss strategies for managing anxiety, and they will advise you to record your thoughts and actions. The most popular methods include:

Tracking down negative thought patterns.

Learning how and why you think the way you do.

Journaling your feelings and ideas.

Generally speaking, a therapist will probe you deeply about your thinking and work to help you see that your pessimistic beliefs are not consistent with reality. They will demonstrate to you that your life isn't as horrible as you believe it to be and that, for the most part, you don't consider all the options before drawing hasty judgments. Additionally, a therapist outlines a few popular mindfulness and meditation-based relaxation techniques. All you need to do is pay attention to your surroundings and feelings rather than spend hours in your room doing yoga or meditation.

Consulting a therapist is not always required. In practical terms, CBT methods are simple self-directed tasks. You are welcome to try CBT if you are not feeling up to seeing a therapist. I advise you to try CBT for several months or maybe a year and then assess the results. It is advised that you see a specialist if you find that you are not improving and that you still have anxiety most of the time. Instead of viewing it as a setback, consider it a chance to learn more about cognitive behavioral therapy and enhance your life. Recall that consulting a therapist is perfectly acceptable.

Advantages OfCbt

CBT offers numerous immediate and long-term advantages. Because CBT procedures are simple and engaging, they keep you intrigued and involved in the short term. Becoming proficient in CBT procedures should only take 15 sessions with a therapist. After that, you'll have all the resources you need to successfully implement CBT techniques in your day-to-day activities. This implies that you will be able to work on your ideas and actions independently. If you practice CBT independently, you may require more time because you may occasionally forget the exercises or make more mistakes. It occurs more readily because you need to exercise greater self-control and determination to practice consistently without having someone assign assignments or provide instructions. This does not, however, mean that you cannot use CBT alone. Just be ready to overcome more barriers and difficulties than you would under the guidance of a therapist. You'll notice benefits extremely soon in every situation. Since you'll realize that you can change your life, you'll also feel more responsible. As a result, you'll be inspired to work even harder to accomplish your objectives. You may reinforce the new concepts you learn and advance more quickly using CBT techniques daily.

You'll observe CBT's long-term impacts after a few months. You'll notice that you don't conduct certain activities as frequently as you once did if you were accustomed to doing them before practicing. Over time, the coping mechanisms you've acquired become instinctive reactions to stressful circumstances, and the practices you've engaged in become ingrained in your routine. If your friend's failure to respond to your messages initially caused you to think negatively, it now causes you to feel indifferent. It requires no effort to generate neutral ideas because they come to you naturally. Because CBT techniques are so effective, you eventually forget about them and integrate them into your everyday routine.

They can live with you for the rest of your life if you practice them consistently for several months and incorporate them into your daily activities. reduce or even stop unhealthy behaviors, handle social settings easily, eliminate unreasonable anxieties and anxiety, and develop self-compassion. CBT methods have a good impact on all areas of your life. They boost your self-assurance in your aptitude to manage a range of circumstances. They also teach you self-care techniques and acknowledge your emotions and senses. They show you that your fears are unneeded and sometimes harmful. To succeed, you need to think positively—not them.

You may be wondering how to guarantee the efficacy of CBT approaches. Well, a lot of studies have been done to determine the true effects of CBT approaches on children, adolescents, and adults, and the findings have consistently been striking. Specifically, disorder (ASD), obsessive-compulsive disorder (OCD), depression, anxiety, and post-traumatic stress disorder (PTSD). Therapists typically advise teenagers with anxiety disorders to practice CBT procedures. To put it another way, CBT is the recommended therapy for treating anxiety.

Additionally, studies have shown that CBT methods provide long-lasting benefits for mental health issues.

Research has also demonstrated that CBT has measurable benefits for social skills, emotional control, and self-esteem. In addition, people who use CBT can curtail harmful or violent behaviors (Friedberg, 2021).

This is presumably the moment where you have eliminated any reservations you may have had regarding the effectiveness of CBT procedures. In any event, you won't be able to reap their numerous advantages and feel better until you give them a try. Simply put, quit overanalyzing and begin using CBT strategies immediately.

Comprehending Anxiety and Stress

Stress: What Is It?

Stress is a strong force that impacts everyone, much as a river's currents shape the terrain it runs through. It's a biological reaction encoded into our systems as a survival mechanism, the body's natural response to any demand or threat. Our bodies go into overdrive when confronted with a stressful scenario, such as an impending deadline, heavy traffic, or a difficult conversation.

Envision yourself facing a snarling, growling creature in the wild. Your muscles strain, your heart quickens, and your senses become more acute. Stress triggers this well-known "fight or flight" reaction. In this case, stress is your body's method of getting ready to flee (fight) or confront (fight) the threat. It's an energy burst that can be fatal under the appropriate conditions.

But unlike wild animals, we don't frequently encounter physical risks in our modern existence. Rather, our bodies frequently respond to psychological or emotional pressures like they would to a life-threatening circumstance, such as marital issues, financial anxieties, or work-related pressure.

Fundamentally, stress is not necessarily harmful. It might spur us to give our best effort and help us accomplish our objectives.

What is the nature of anxiety?

Conversely, anxiety is like the constant hum of a background noise that never really goes away. Anticipating future events—whether they be viewed as threats or not—often sets it off. Anxiety, in contrast to stress, is often a chronic feeling of uneasiness and trepidation rather than an acute and instantaneous reaction.

Consider anxiety as your mind warning you about possible threats. It serves as a mental alarm system, alerting you to potential problems and assisting in your preparation. A certain amount of anxiety is acceptable and even beneficial, but persistent anxiety can be crippling.

"What if" questions are a common way that anxiety shows up: What if I fail? What if something negative occurs? What if others judge me? These thoughts can be unbearable, leading to bodily symptoms like shaky hands, a racing heart, restlessness, and irritation.

The Relationship Between Anxiety and Stress

Anxiety and stress are closely related, like the threads of a tapestry woven into the fabric of our lives; they are not distinct entities. Anxiety can intensify stress, while stress can be exacerbated by anxiety.

For instance, pressure from a high-stress level at work may cause you to have uneasy thoughts about your performance, job security, or capacity for coping. A vicious cycle of anxiety and tension can result from these unsettling ideas.

It is critical to comprehend this relationship since it emphasizes how critical stress and anxiety management are to preserving general well-being. We'll go into greater detail about these intricate feelings in the upcoming chapters, examining how they impact your body and mind and give you the skills you need to regain control of your life. Remind yourself that you can change how you relate to stress and anxiety, turning them from overwhelming enemies into tame allies on your path to a more tranquil and balanced life.

In Conclusion: The Path To Completeness

Amidst dread, anxiety, and despair, you embarked on a profound journey of healing, transformation, and spiritual development. Along the way, you leaned on the strength of prayer and the wisdom of scripture, finding comfort and strength in embracing religion. You become adept at maintaining your inner calm and creating a safe refuge amid adversity. At last, you discovered a fulfilling and significant life.

This path has not been without difficulties but has also seen profound growth, insight, and renewal periods.

You now understand that overcoming fear, worry, and sadness involves more than just letting go of these mental burdens; it also entails growing in intimacy with God and realizing the effectiveness of prayer.

Remember that as you advance, your journey toward completion is never-ending. It's a dynamic process of continuing growth, spiritual expansion, and self-discovery. It proves your perseverance, unshakable faith, and capacity to find happiness and meaning amid adversity.

Embrace every day as a new opportunity to deepen your faith, discover inner serenity, and lead a life that reflects your passions and convictions. The Divine presence travels by you on this road, offering guidance, love, and support so you are never alone.

May your life serve as a testament to the transformative power of faith, the grace of prayer for healing, and the many opportunities that arise from living a life that is fulfilled and in line with your purpose. May you find peace, courage, and deep joy in embracing your faith. May you also radiate the light of hope to those who travel similar paths.

Wholeness is a sacred route; you are the brave and determined traveler on it. May you always have an open heart to the wonder and beauty of life's many possibilities, and may the freedom from facing your fears, accepting inner peace, and having faith in yourself cause your soul to soar.

Conscientious Meditation

Women are aware of the debilitating nature of anxiety. In addition to therapy and medication, there are various strategies for managing anxiety symptoms. One well-liked method for enhancing mental wellness is mindfulness meditation, which has several advantages.

Being judgment-free in the present moment is a key component of mindfulness meditation. In this chapter, we will look at a few mindful awareness techniques specially meant to assist women in overcoming anxiety.

The body scan meditation is one effective activity. Lying down, closing your eyes, and concentrating on each body part—from your toes to your head—is a straightforward yet deep technique. Pay attention to each bodily area and notice, without passing judgment, any sensations that surface, such as discomfort, tension, or relaxation.

You may relax your mind and eliminate tension from your body by doing this exercise daily. It's an effective strategy that can make you feel more in the moment and anchored in your everyday existence. Now, let's get started and discover how to include body scan meditation in your daily practice for mental wellness.

The advantages of practicing mindfulness meditation

Anxiety spins a complex web deep within our minds, entangling our ideas and strengthening our hold on our emotions. Women have particular difficulties that can add to the crippling weight of anxiety. But do not be alarmed; you possess a remarkable ability just waiting to be released. You can discover your inner power through mindfulness meditation, a technique that can lead you on a transforming journey toward mental well-being.

A deeply personal journey that encourages you to welcome the present moment with an open heart and nonjudgmental gaze, mindfulness meditation is more than just a method. You will find comfort and release from the anxiety-inducing bonds that have imprisoned you for far too long in this haven of self-discovery. Together, let's walk along this empowering path and allow me to share the many advantages of mindfulness meditation.

Reduces Stress: Visualize yourself floating in a serene sanctuary, where stress disappears like morning mist beneath the sun's soft rays. We trigger our relaxation response when we practice mindfulness meditation. Our blood pressure drops, our heart rate lowers, and the sneaky cortisol levels fall. Anxiety's hold weakens when stress recedes and is replaced by a peaceful serenity that permeates our entire being. Enhances Emotional Regulation: The storm of emotional turmoil is located inside the maze of anxiety. It's a trip full of whirlpools of volatile emotions and erratic tides. But do not be alarmed; mindfulness meditation provides the compass you need to navigate this turbulent sea. You can successfully traverse complex emotional pathways by developing self-awareness and self-control. Acknowledge their ebb and flow, comprehend their source, and react to them with tact and empathy.

Rises Resilience: Although life's storms may rock us to our very core, there is an unwavering strength inside that is just waiting to be discovered. This buried resilience within us is revealed through mindfulness meditation. We may overcome adversity with grace and wisdom when we bring light to our ideas and feelings. We develop a strong, robust spirit along this path, strengthened by self-awareness and equipped with the means to weather any storm that comes our way.

Enhances Sleep Quality: We no longer have to suffer through the sleepless evenings when sleeplessness and worry dance together. We can enter a state of calm sleep with the help of mindfulness meditation. Sleep becomes a haven where tranquility blooms as tension fades and relaxation takes over. Allow your racing mind to fade and be replaced by a peaceful serenity that lulls you into a comfortable embrace.

Improves Well-being: Women are naturally good caregivers, frequently putting their needs last. We are encouraged by mindfulness meditation to value self-care, accept self-awareness, and show ourselves a lot of kindness. We become aware of our ideas, emotions, and bodily experiences within this elevated awareness.

With this newfound consciousness, we discover how to gently and gracefully care for our well-being. It is only through developing a loving relationship with ourselves that we can overcome anxiety and welcome an endlessly joyful life.

Recall that mindfulness meditation is a long-term practice that calls for perseverance, commitment, and consistency rather than a quick cure for worry.

Observant respiration

Deep down in the pit of my nervous psyche, I longed for a lifeline, some basic yet profound method that would calm and soothe my restless spirit. I later learned about the transforming potential of mindful breathing. This age-old method, which has been passed down through the ages, contained the secret to releasing anxiety's bonds and showing the way to mental health. Allow me to guide you on a personal exploration of your breath, where we will learn about the many advantages that mindful breathing has to offer.

More than just a method, mindful breathing is a personal dance with the very essence of life. I took solace in the here and now when I adopted this practice, using my breath as my anchor. I let the physical feelings dance inside me with every breath in and out. My senses were filled with the rising and falling of my chest, the soft brushing of air through my nostrils, and the musical symphony of my breath. I learned to be a judgment- and expectation-free observer of my thoughts, feelings, and bodily sensations in this hallowed place.

Because mindful breathing activates the parasympathetic nerve system, which is in charge of our body's relaxation response, it is an extremely effective tool in the fight against anxiety.

Our sympathetic nervous system takes over during stressful and anxious periods, spiking stress hormones and adrenaline to prime our bodies for a fight-or-flight reaction. But we may overcome this instinctive response by engaging in mindful breathing, which opens the door to peace and profound relaxation.

The flexibility of attentive breathing is what makes it so beautiful. It can be embraced in many ways and customized to fit our unique lifestyles and preferences. Some people find comfort in creating a peaceful haven where they may spend a few priceless minutes daily concentrating only on breathing. Some people find it easy to incorporate mindful breathing into their everyday schedules, finding moments of calm among the chaos of household duties or the morning commute. Breathing exercises and guided meditations, easily accessible online or via mindfulness applications, can also be companions on this journey.

Exposing the Harmony of Signs

Each person affected by ADHD has a different experience because of the combination of symptoms that frequently work in unison to form a sound.

1. Inattentiveness: The hallmark of ADHD is inattentiveness, which manifests as a propensity for daydreaming, difficulty focusing or maintaining attention on tasks, and a lack of detail awareness that leads to careless mistakes. Simple instructions could be overlooked, making time management and planning challenging.

2. Hyperactivity: Characterized by worry, hyperactivity is a constant want to move. ADHD sufferers may have trouble staying still, moving around a lot, or tapping their feet. This characteristic can make people anxious at pivotal

moments, impacting interpersonal and professional contexts.

3. Impulsivity: When an ADHD person exhibits impulsivity, they frequently make impulsive decisions without thinking through the consequences. Common signs include talking too much, acting dangerously, and interrupting others. Because impulsivity might give the impression that one is disregarding the thoughts or feelings of others, it can strain relationships.

Putting Shared Responsibilities in Motion: The Balancing Act

The coordination of movements is an essential component of any dance. This alignment, like a well-choreographed pattern, frequently requires careful balancing in a relationship impacted by ADHD.

1. Managing Responsibilities

Having ADHD can make task management feel like a balancing act. It is possible for domestic chores, bill payments, and scheduling appointments to be neglected or abandoned, necessitating a greater involvement from the non-ADHD spouse in these areas.

2. Deciding on the Proper Pace

Setting up a consistent schedule and tempo becomes crucial. Both spouses must strike a balance so that the ADHD partner can develop and significant responsibilities are completed and distributed equally.

3. Adjusting to Shifting Tempos

Task dancing might not have a predictable rhythm. Because of its erratic nature, ADHD can cause people to adjust to shifting beats and be flexible in redistributing tasks according to their partner's capacity and present state of focus.

The Dance of Closeness

Any relationship starts with intimacy, a dance of emotional connection, openness, and trust. This pas de deux is made more difficult by ADHD.

Finding the Correct Balance:

A careful balance between physical separation and mental connection is necessary for intimacy. It can be difficult for a spouse with ADHD to find this balance at times, which could lead to mental space or overwhelm the other with intense emotions.

2. The Attention Choreography:

A fundamental component of proximity is attention. Due to ADHD's impact on attention, partners may need to develop new strategies to maintain emotional connection and focus.

3. Encouraging the Understanding of Dance

In this cautious dance, understanding must be fostered. To help each other maintain a solid emotional bond, both partners need to put in the time and effort to comprehend the special difficulties that ADHD brings and adjust their behavior.

The aspects of a couple's lives that ADHD impacts are similar to a complicated dance that calls for tolerance, understanding, and a willingness to change. In this dance, partners practice synchronizing their movements while appreciating the special beat ADHD adds to their union. Partners can navigate the challenges of managing a relationship while dealing with the complex rhythms of ADHD by acknowledging and accepting this dance.

Developing Resilience

Prioritizing the development of a solid support network is one of the finest strategies to increase resilience. Having good relationships with loved ones, family, and friends is a part of this. Self-care is another essential element of resilience.

Resilience can be developed via self-compassion, self-care, and a solid support network. Being gentle and patient with oneself instead of being judgmental is a sign of self-compassion. This entails admitting your limitations, acknowledging your skills, and being willing to learn from your failures.

Concentrating on the things you can control instead of the ones you can't is another strategy for developing resilience. While many circumstances in life are beyond our control, it's crucial to concentrate on the things we can affect and change. For instance, concentrate on what you can do to prepare for or better a situation rather than fretting about how it will turn out.

Discovering a sense of direction and significance in life is among the finest strategies to develop resilience. Even in trying circumstances, having a purpose in life can help you stay motivated and have a sense of direction. This can be going after a fulfilling profession, taking up a pastime, or spending time with close friends and family.

Building Resilience Capabilities

Resilience is crucial for handling stress, overcoming obstacles, and preserving mental and emotional health. Resilience is the ability to overcome hardship, adjust to change, and become stronger in adversity. It's a talent that may be developed and enhanced with time. Let's take a closer look at the essential elements of building resilience skills:

Positive Thinking: - Even in trying circumstances, maintain a positive frame of mind by emphasizing your blessings, opportunities, and strengths.

- Use strategies like cognitive restructuring, which replaces illogical ideas with more reasonable ones, to combat negative thoughts and cognitive distortions.

Emotional Regulation: Acquire emotional intelligence by recognizing, comprehending, and controlling your feelings.

To lessen emotional reactivity and preserve balance, engage in mindfulness and relaxation practices.

Problem-Solving: - Develop your problem-solving ability by decomposing difficulties into doable steps and creating original solutions.

- Take action and make decisions, even modest ones, to avoid overanalyzing and dwelling on the past.

Flexibility & Adaptability: Acknowledge change as a necessary aspect of life and cultivate the capacity to adjust to novel situations and obstacles.

- Keep an open mind and view failures as chances for personal improvement.

Social Support: - Have a solid network of friends and family who offer practical and emotional support when things get hard.

- When necessary, seek professional assistance, such as counseling or therapy.

Self-Care: - Make self-care routines a priority. These include getting enough sleep, eating a healthy diet, exercising frequently, and practicing relaxation.

- Take part in enjoyable activities that make you feel happy and fulfilled.

Develop a resilient mindset by seeing failures as transitory, not reflecting your value or aptitude.

- Practice self-compassion and be kind and understanding to oneself, even when things are tough.

Goal Setting and Vision: - Establish definite, attainable objectives that provide direction and a feeling of purpose. Setting objectives can inspire you and give you a sense of success.

- Develop a vision for the future and rely on it to motivate and inspire you.

Looking for a Purpose and Meaning:

Consider your principles and the things that bring purpose to your life. Connect with your goal to discover inspiration and fortitude in the face of difficulty.

- Take part in pursuits that fulfill you and are consistent with your principles.

The Anxiety Powder

This chapter aims to provide you with a clear understanding of social anxiety. To do this, you will examine what social anxiety is and is not (such as commonplace uneasiness and shyness) and the characteristics of social anxiety, including its causes, symptoms, indicators, and hazards. You will require all this crucial information when you embark on your recovery process.

ANXIETY NOTHING

Let's take a step back and clarify what anxiety is not before you start studying everything there is to know about social anxiety. In this manner, you won't become confused when you learn more about anxiety in the future. It's simple to confuse anxiety with other emotions or to mistake certain feelings for anxiety. Let's now distinguish between anxiety and the two typical emotions that are sometimes mistaken for it. Shyness and anxiety daily are these two feelings.

Everyone has occasional moments of anxiety. However, it might be challenging to distinguish between anxiety and nervousness if you don't fully grasp each idea. The primary distinction is that anxiety is a medical disease that can be diagnosed, whereas nervousness is a common emotion that everyone experiences daily. Anxiety is characterized by feelings of excitement, worry, or even mild fear, and a particular event typically triggers it. Conversely, anxiety is characterized by intense fear and worry over a wide range of possible problems. An additional distinction is that anxiety is a transient state of mind. Your anxiety goes away as soon as the trigger situation is resolved. However, anxiety is a chronic illness. You might worry about your anxiety-inducing situation even after you've resolved your current source of worry. Alternately, you'll begin to worry about the following scenario. Once the cause of the anxiety is addressed, it persists. Rather, it pertains to other aspects of your existence. If you're anxious, you'll be able to get over your anxiety eventually. If you suffer from anxiety, you will experience anxiety nearly every day and find it difficult to remember when you were completely at ease. Since nervousness frequently reacts to something specific, you can utilize it to your advantage. Your anxiousness acts as a warning system for things that could be hazardous. Although unpleasant, you should pay attention to it because it's essentially trying to assist you. And your anxiety will subside as soon as you take action to lessen the situation's threat or danger. This implies that your anxiety serves mainly to protect you. In the meantime, anxiousness is a sickness that strikes in fits and starts without waiting for a particular occasion to set it off. It will just make you feel nervous all the time. Furthermore, the likelihood is that your fear is not a practical or sensible concern, even if it is focused on a particular event. As a result, your anxiety is pointless and simply serves to cause you unnecessary emotional suffering.

Anxiety differs greatly from normal anxiousness in that it can result in negative thoughts. You will be more focused on the constructive steps you can take to enhance your circumstances and ease your anxiety because anxiety is centered on a particular event that you can alter to lessen it. But anxiety isn't always concentrated on one thing, and even when it is, it's not necessarily something you can control or make better. You will be suspended in inaction by this nebulous anguish over something you cannot control, and you will unavoidably start to give more attention to your thoughts than your actions. Furthermore, anxiety can cause such excruciating pain and unpleasantness that it can send your thoughts to some very dark and challenging areas. To deal with your anxiety, this might subsequently result in maladaptive behaviors like self-harm or other self-damaging acts (such as drinking, smoking, or gambling). In the worst circumstances of anxiety, your suicidal thoughts may even arise because your anxiety has gotten so bad that you believe there is no other way out of it. Your anxiousness may be the source of persistent, all-consuming, gloomy thoughts. Another distinction between worry and nervousness is that anxiety has the potential to disrupt one's life. Since anxiety is fleeting, you can deal with it and carry on with your life with ease. Even though you may be anxious about performing some activities, you can typically do them despite your anxiety. However, when you have anxiety, your feelings could be so strong that they prevent you from taking action on your worries. This may severely disrupt your daily life. Your worry may force you to start avoiding situations that give you discomfort, to miss out on opportunities, or to ruin particular relationships. Your life may be severely limited and harmed by all of this. You will be so overcome with anxiety that you will miss out on a lot of activities or feel incapable of doing them.

Furthermore, despite the common misconception that it is, social anxiety is not the same as shyness. This could be the reason why many who suffer from social anxiety seldom get treatment—they may not be aware that they have a diagnosable mental illness. To assist you in differentiating between the two, let's examine the precise definition of shyness. A feeling of unease or anxiety typically brought on by a fear of social situations is known as shyness. Low self-esteem, excessive self-consciousness, poor self-evaluations, and negative self-preoccupations are frequently associated with shyness. Being shy can be defined as being guarded and shy around strangers, in unfamiliar settings, or while approaching or being approached by someone you know. Common symptoms of shyness include low self-esteem, anxiety about what others think of you, a strong desire to retreat or avoid social situations, blushing, perspiration, elevated heart rate, and stomach problems.

Shyness might have a few different reasons. A low feeling of self-worth is the first. The indications and manifestations of shyness you have read about above relate to self-concept. In other words, how you view, value, feel about, assess, and are preoccupied with yourself. You wouldn't be overly self-conscious or self-preoccupied, have reasonable self-evaluations, and have a positive sense of who you are. All of this comes together to create a confident and well-balanced person. However, all these qualities will be harmed and unhealthy if you don't feel good about yourself. As a result, you can start to lose your confidence and become timid. A person's sense of self is shaped by many elements, including genetics, environment, and parenting, and it begins to take shape in childhood. That is to say, shyness is not innate in you.

Instead, shyness develops within you in the same way as any other characteristic. There are more biological and environmental variables that contribute to shyness. Your social contacts with your parents, in particular, might significantly impact your shyness levels. Overly protective parents may unintentionally cause their kids to grow up timid, lack confidence, and struggle with social skills. These parents may never let their kids go out independently, make errors, and stand independently. As a result, the kids never have the chance to develop self-confidence. This may result in a poor sense of self and extreme timidity.

Now, contrast this description with the one above. Anxiety disorders that include fear or apprehension about social circumstances and performance are known as social anxiety disorders. A person suffering from social anxiety may experience fear or worry when speaking in front of an audience, participating in meetings or classes, making new friends, attending social gatherings or events, answering a chance call, or voicing their ideas to others. Exposure to judgment, criticism, scrutiny, or rejection in a social or performance setting is the primary theme of worry for those with social anxiety. Feelings of humiliation or embarrassment, fear of interacting with strangers, excessive performance analysis, being overly critical of oneself, avoiding situations where one might end up the center of attention, blushing, elevated heart rate, trembling, dizziness, or stomach problems are common indications and symptoms of social anxiety. Still, this is merely a shortened, streamlined list of symptoms. The following section will have a longer list.

Similarly, the following is a condensed list of possible reasons for social anxiety. Similar to shyness, social anxiety is a condition that develops inside of you as a result of several interrelated factors rather than something innate. In addition to contextual elements like the social contacts you have during the developing years, genetics also plays a part. For instance, your chances of getting social anxiety may be higher if you were raised in a controlling or overly protective atmosphere. The same may be stated if you were raised in a home where there was abuse, bullying, parent divorce, or family strife. These unpleasant encounters may cause you to develop social anxiety.

Section I: Examining Anxiety

Anxiety Disorder Types

Anxiety Disorder in General (GAD)

GAD is one of the most prevalent anxiety diseases, affecting millions of individuals worldwide. An inability to regulate worried thoughts and sentiments over commonplace, everyday events is what defines it. GAD sufferers may find it difficult to control their anxiety, which can result in symptoms including agitation, stiffness in the muscles, and difficulty focusing. Anxiety frequently lasts longer than the initial stressful incident and can extend to many other aspects of life, including relationships, employment, health, and finances. The crippling consequences of GAD symptoms can make daily living extremely difficult.

Disorder of Social Anxiety (SAD)

The core of social anxiety disorder, also referred to as social phobia, is an overwhelming fear of social situations and other people's attention. People who have social anxiety disorder (SAD) usually fear being embarrassed or judged, which makes them avoid social situations or experience them in great discomfort. This fear is not limited to unfamiliar situations; common social interactions, such as giving a speech in front of an audience or going to social gatherings, can cause extreme anxiety. Certain social situations might cause physical symptoms like flushing, shaking, or sweating, which can amplify the anxiety felt.

Anxiety Disorder

Acute episodes of intense anxiety and discomfort lasting a few minutes are the main features of panic disorder. Great fear of experiencing another panic attack following a very bad one. An attack can cause several symptoms, including dizziness, shortness of breath, chest pain, palpitations, and a debilitating sense of fear. The fear of another panic attack can hurt an individual's quality of life.

Fear of spiders

Anxiety sufferers frequently use avoiding circumstances like elevators where they could feel trapped as a coping method. Engaging in daily activities and social interactions could be challenging when someone acts this way.

Particular Fears

An extreme and illogical fear of a single object or situation is a defining feature of a specific phobia. While arachnophobia is a fear of spiders, aviophobia is a fear of flying, trypanophobia is a fear of needles, and acrophobia is a fear of heights. Some phobics will take great pains to keep their triggers hidden from them because they are so afraid of them. Some phobias can significantly interfere with day-to-day functioning, making it difficult to socialize or go to work.

OCD, or obsessive-compulsive disorder Compulsive-Obsessive People with this illness experience both compulsions, which are repetitive, undesired, and relaxing behavioral or mental acts, and obsessions, which are painful thoughts, ideas, or desires. Ideas of infection, harm, or the quest for perfection are common themes in obsessions.

Compulsions include things like counting, checking, and excessive hand washing. Many OCD sufferers are self-aware enough to know that their compulsions and obsessions go beyond what is required to lessen their anxiety, but they nonetheless indulge in them.

PTSD, or post-traumatic stress disorder Post-stressful Stress Disorder can result from exposure to stressful experiences such as sexual assault, war, or even a significant accident. Post-traumatic stress disorder symptoms include increased awareness, emotional numbness, nightmares, and flashbacks. Those with post-traumatic stress disorder (PTSD) may experience severe emotional distress and functional impairment when reminded of the incident. Post-traumatic stress disorder may not always result from trauma, and each individual may experience the illness differently in terms of severity and length.

Disorder of Separation Anxiety

Separation anxiety is more frequent among children, but it can also affect adults. An unreasonable fear of being separated from close ones or safe havens like one's own home is what defines it. Due to these concerns, people may avoid relationships and activities that could lead to separation.

In most contexts, people with selective mutism can communicate properly, but when they are in social situations when they need to interact with others, they become non-communicative. People suffering from this illness may find it difficult to communicate, which could hurt their social and academic lives.

Particular Anxiety Diseases in Children

In addition to the diseases mentioned above, children may also have anxiety disorders specific to their age and developmental stage. SAD, SM and other phobias like those of animals or the dark are possible examples. It's critical to identify and address childhood anxiety as soon as possible because doing so may prevent more severe problems in the future. Anxiety is experienced differently by each individual, and these disorders are indicative of that. While each anxiety disorder has its unique collection of symptoms and diagnostic standards, they are all characterized by a substantial impairment in daily functioning and quality of life. The first step toward conquering the challenges brought on by anxiety in contemporary life is acknowledging these issues and seeking support.

Recognizing Mental Congestion.

An abundance of ideas, thoughts, or information in the mind can cause mental clutter, impairing concentration, decision-making, and clear thinking. It can be brought on by stress, concern, multitasking, excessive stimuli, or unresolved issues, which makes it challenging to set priorities and arrange ideas effectively.

Many live their lives feeling weighted down, unable to focus clearly, and generally stressed without truly understanding why in our increasingly busy and connected society.

Therefore, it's important to recognize mental clutter as the surplus of ideas and thoughts that clog your mind and make it difficult for you to concentrate or think clearly about the task. It can make you hyperactive, drain your vitality, and feel heavy.

It is possible to experience worry, stress, anxiety, negative thinking, and any other type of intrusive or unwelcome thinking in addition to this overpowering feeling of having too much on your mind. Furthermore, it can come from various places, including personal relationships, social media, the workplace, and family. Although the research behind mental clutter is still developing, we do know that it can negatively affect our thoughts, emotions, and quality of life.

We often pass this off as a normal part of life and attribute it to busyness or "the grind." Indeed, life changes or external stressors can cause mental congestion. But a great deal of mental clutter is self-inflicted. Fortunately, it's also fixable by yourself.

❖ Trying to stay ahead of the Jones family

One of the main reasons for clutter is the desire to stay up to date with our neighbors, friends, and family. Even when we don't need certain items, we could feel pressured to buy them to "keep up with the Joneses." It's easy to think that simply because someone else owns a certain product or brand, we should, too. But instead of making impulsive purchases, we should stop and consider whether they would improve our lives and whether they are necessary.

❖ The effects of marketing and advertising

Marketing, advertising, and promotion may entice us to purchase items we don't truly need.

It's important to consider advertising messages while making a purchase decision. When purchasing, we should be aware of deceptive strategies like "limited-time specials" and "buy now or miss out" sales techniques.

◻ Views of society on wealth and achievement:

Things now almost automatically equate to success. For example, having a fancy car or stylish clothing can give the impression that a person is successful and wealthy.

However, this is a false belief, and if we feel that we must acquire more stuff to succeed, then this is a major contributor to clutter. Rather, it is imperative to recognize that genuine achievement stems from diligence and commitment rather than acquiring material possessions or adhering to vogue.

Third, Environmental Aspects

Storage for the home● Living in small quarters

Living in a tiny place with more possessions than you can fit in might worsen clutter. Your belongings can quickly accumulate and take over your house if you don't have enough storage space.

This problem is particularly common in cities, where many people reside in compact apartments with limited space for storage.

People without access to filing cabinets, shelving, and other storage options usually find it difficult to keep their belongings organized.

It is hard to distinguish between items that need to be kept outside and those that can be stored when loose commodities are kept out in the open without storage.

● Unfinished projects

Unfinished jobs are a common source of clutter. Unfinished projects, like an old book you meant to read or furniture you meant to assemble, frequently occupy physical space in our homes but don't accomplish anything.

To prevent the items from becoming clutter, make sure that any undone tasks are either finished or thrown away.

● Cohabiting with an overwhelming amount of people

You will not throw your husband out of the house; therefore, it's not something you can change. However, living in a tiny location with too many people can quickly result in clutter. Additionally, it might be challenging to devise a system that benefits everyone when everyone operates according to their own set of procedures.

The significance of living in the present

It is easy to get mired in the past or fret about the future in today's fast-paced, constantly-evolving world. Our mental and physical health can benefit greatly from learning to live in the present.

The following justifies the significance of being present and how it might lead to a more satisfying life:

Enhanced drive and vitality: We can become more energized and motivated to accomplish our goals by focusing on the here and now.

We are more likely to participate in and enjoy the process when focused on the task at hand, increasing output and satisfaction.

Better Relationships: Being present broadens our awareness of our environment and helps us listen to our loved ones more intently. Stronger, deeper connections result from our ability to connect with people and comprehend their needs when engaged in fully present encounters.

Increased happiness: Studies have shown that living in the present moment might increase our level of happiness. We may live happier, more contented lives daily if we appreciate where we live and allow ourselves to enjoy ourselves.

Decreased stress and anxiety: Our personal and professional lives suffer when we are not living in the present. Distracted behavior at work can lead to more mistakes and the loss of important cues from others that could facilitate cooperation or prevent needless conflict. We can reduce tension and abrupt mood swings because we have more control over our thoughts in the present.

Increased attention and concentration: Being present benefits our abilities to pay attention, focus, learn, listen, and remember things. By connecting with ourselves and the world around us, this attentiveness enables us to notice the little things in life and makes sure we don't "miss anything."

Increased self-awareness:

A stronger sense of control over our lives, better decision-making, and problem-solving abilities can all be brought about by this heightened self-awareness.

Improved physical health: Research has indicated that living in the present moment can benefit one's physical well-being.

Engaging completely in our activities also allows us to make better decisions, like eating attentively and working out frequently.

Increased Creativity:

We create mental room to consider fresh concepts and viewpoints when we let go of worry about the past and the future.

A stronger sense of purpose and fulfillment can be attained by living in the present moment and giving our jobs, interests, and relationships our whole attention.

We can truly appreciate and enjoy the present and make the most of every moment when we are not preoccupied with thoughts of the past or the future.

Better decision-making: By considering all pertinent information and efficiently assessing the advantages and disadvantages, being present helps us make better judgments.

We can focus on the task at hand and make decisions that are consistent with our beliefs and aspirations when we are not sidetracked by regrets from the past or anxieties about the future.

Improved time management: By prioritizing work, establishing reasonable goals, and avoiding procrastination, we may make the most of our time when present. We can operate more productively and efficiently by concentrating on one task at a time, which reduces stress and increases our sense of accomplishment.

A stronger bond with nature: Spending time in nature can significantly impact our well-being. Some advantages include less stress, improved mood, and an increased sense of wonder and admiration.

Our connection to the natural world and all living things can be strengthened by taking the time to appreciate its beauty and complexity.

So let's reserve a few days in a strange place, prepare our belongings, and relish the feeling of sudden transformation.

Simply tell yourself, "I'll get over anything, no matter what happens." I play that game!"

www.ingramcontent.com/pod-product-compliance
Lightning Source LLC
Chambersburg PA
CBHW052137110526
44591CB00012B/1752